No Lex 10-12

written in 1-29-98cc

Elvis Presley

Vanora Leigh

Illustrated by Richard Hook

The Bookwright Press
New York · 1986

Great Lives

William Shakespeare
Queen Elizabeth II
Anne Frank
Martin Luther King, Jr.
Helen Keller
Ferdinand Magellan
Mother Teresa
Louis Braille
John Lennon
John F. Kennedy
Florence Nightingale
Elvis Presley

First published in the
United States in 1986 by
The Bookwright Press
387 Park Avenue South
New York, NY 10016

First published in 1986 by
Wayland (Publishers) Limited
61 Western Road, Hove
East Sussex BN3 1JD, England

ISBN 0–531–15073–5
Library of Congress Card Number: 85–73674

Phototypeset by Kalligraphics Ltd, Redhill, Surrey
Printed in Italy by G. Canale & C.S.p.A., Turin

Contents

The "King" of Rock 'n' Roll

A major newspaper recently published a glowing review of an Elvis Presley album, describing him as "a remarkable artist." It seems that people are still fascinated by Elvis. When he was alive, he was one of the most famous men in the world. Even in death he has remained a legend.

Elvis has often been called a true working-class hero. He was born into a life of great poverty, yet by the time he was twenty years old he had become a household name. He was the first white singer who not only sounded like a black singer but was actually not afraid to sound like one. Coming from the racially prejudiced Deep South of the United States, this was a daring achievement, both professionally and personally. Elvis opened the door to a new and exciting form of music which would be enjoyed by millions of people all over the world.

Elvis went from being nicknamed "Elvis the Pelvis" to becoming the undisputed "King" of Rock 'n' Roll. No one ever tried to steal that title – the world's most famous performers acknowledged Elvis as the "King." At the height of their success, the Beatles praised Elvis. "If there hadn't been an Elvis, there wouldn't have been the Beatles," said John Lennon.

Elvis' life was a success story beyond anyone's wildest imaginings. But it was also a sad tale; a warning of how fame, unless carefully handled, can finally destroy a person.

Elvis rehearsing before a concert.

An only child

Elvis Presley's parents, Gladys and Vernon, were married in 1933, when she was twenty-one and he was seventeen. They lived in Tupelo, Mississippi, a small town not far from Memphis in the Deep South. It was here, two years later, on January 8, 1935, that their son Elvis Aaron was born, one of a pair of twins. Sad to say, the other twin was stillborn.

The Presleys were a very poor family. The United States was in the middle of the Great Depression and many people

As a young child, Elvis lived in a wooden shack with his family in Tupelo.

were unemployed or trying to exist on meagre wages. Elvis was brought up in a two-room wooden shack but his parents made sure he was not deprived in any way, and that he grew up a healthy boy. They were a religious family and attended church regularly. It was here that Elvis first showed an interest in music by trying to join in with the choir when they were gospel singing when he was just two years old!

Elvis' talent for singing was not recognized by anyone, apart from his parents, until he was eight years old. Then a teacher at his school heard him singing a song about a boy and his dog, *Old Shep,* and was so impressed that Elvis was entered for a children's talent competition at the annual Mississippi-Alabama Agricultural Fair. He won second prize.

Like most boys, Elvis always wanted a bicycle and asked if he could have one for his eleventh birthday. But the Presleys were so poor that they had to leave their home, and were now living with relatives. The family could not afford to buy a bicycle, so they bought their son a guitar instead. Elvis took his guitar with him everywhere he went. He managed to teach himself to play by listening to records and the radio, enjoying, in particular, the rhythm and blues performed by black musicians. Elvis later described his self-taught style of playing and the sound he made as like "someone beating on a bucket lid!"

Moving on

When Elvis was thirteen, the family moved to Memphis so that Vernon Presley could find regular work. "We were broke, man, broke," Elvis later remembered. But when they reached Memphis, prospects did not look any brighter than they had before. Again, the Presleys found themselves living in the poorest housing, in the poorest part of town.

Elvis was overwhelmed by his new school, Humes High, which had 1,700 students. He ran away on his first day, but returned the next day and settled in, although he was always a quiet, rather lonely teenager. His mother, Gladys, still adored her son and continued to accompany him to school!

Gradually the family finances improved. Vernon and Gladys both found regular jobs. When Gladys became ill, Elvis took a part-time job in a movie house, showing people to their seats. He

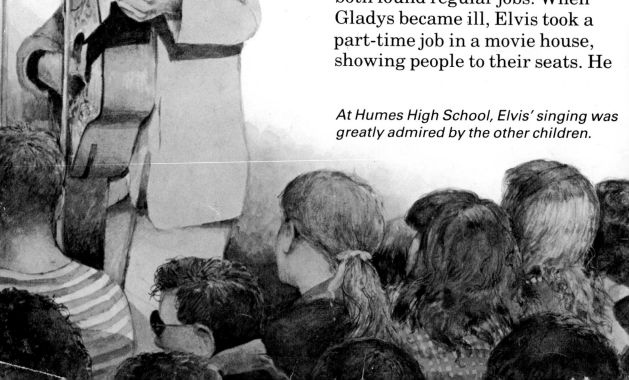

At Humes High School, Elvis' singing was greatly admired by the other children.

lost the job when he was discovered watching the films instead of working!

Elvis did not attract much attention at school, and he tried to impress the other children by wearing bright clothes and growing his hair long. "I wasn't popular in school," he later admitted, adding that he did not even have a girlfriend then! Only once did Elvis make his mark, at a school concert, when his singing had his classmates shouting for more.

Elvis spent most of his spare time strumming his guitar, although he rarely played in public. He liked to visit Beale Street, in Memphis, where he could listen to the black musicians who influenced his own style of music so much.

Yet at eighteen, Elvis had no ambitions to be a professional musician. After leaving school, he got a job as a truck driver and earned a good wage of $42 a week. Vernon Presley had spent most of his life driving trucks and most people assumed that his son would do the same.

Elvis loved listening to the black musicians on Beale Street.

A present for Gladys

Even when Elvis was a grown man, he was still very much a "mother's boy." Elvis and Gladys had a close relationship, and at the height of his fame he called her "my best girl."

It was because of Gladys that Elvis unknowingly took the first step towards fame and fortune. For her birthday in 1953, he gave her a record of himself singing. The Memphis Recording Service allowed anyone to make a record for just $4. Elvis sang two ballads, *My Happiness* and *That's When Your Heartaches Begin*.

Gladys loved her record and played it until it was worn out!

A young secretary at the Sun Record company, of which the Memphis Recording Service was a part, played Elvis' recording to her boss, Sam Phillips. Sun Records had recorded many famous blues musicians but, because of racial prejudice, these recordings by black men and women were never bought by white people in the Deep South. Sam's ambition was to find a white singer who sounded like a black singer. Then the large white population would buy the records and make Sam very rich.

At first, when Sam heard Elvis on tape, he was not very interested. In 1954, Elvis returned to make another recording and this time he met Sam. Sam later remembered "the singer with the sideburns," and asked Elvis to come over to the studios. Sam was impressed, and arranged for Elvis to play with other musicians for the first time.

The record that emerged from these sessions was made while Elvis and the other musicians were having a break, playing for their own amusement. On one side was a blues number, *That's*

Elvis began his film-acting career in 1956 with Love Me Tender.

All Right and on the other *Blue Moon of Kentucky*. This record was played by local radio stations and soon sold over 20,000 copies in the Memphis district alone.

"The Hillbilly Cat"

The success of Elvis' first record meant that he and his backing group, Scotty Moore and Bill Black, were much in demand for live performances. Elvis became known as the "Hillbilly Cat," and

This teenager was overcome with emotion at an Elvis concert.

Scotty and Bill as the "Blue Moon Boys." During much of 1954 and 1955, they performed all over Mississippi and Texas.

Elvis created a sensation wherever he appeared, because of his singing and his movements on stage. While other singers stood still at the microphone, Elvis did the splits, swiveled his hips and fell on his knees. Some people were shocked by these performances but the girls loved him.

As well as traveling, Elvis made four more records for the Sun label, all a combination of blues on one side and country music on the other. As the recordings gained popularity and Elvis began to acquire a cult following, it became clear that such a show-stopper had the potential to become a nationally famous entertainer.

Elvis was certainly ambitious, but he needed someone with knowledge and influence who could make him known outside the South. Colonel Tom Parker, who had spent many years managing and publicizing

The "Blue Moon Boys" were Elvis' first backing group.

various entertainers, recognized Elvis' talent as being quite exceptional. "This boy will go far," he said.

Tom Parker took over the role of Elvis' manager and began to promote him in the autumn of 1955. He presented his protégé to the DJs assembled for the Country and Western Disc Jockey Convention, and Elvis was voted the Most Promising Newcomer of the Year. Colonel Parker also realized that Elvis needed to move away from a small record company like Sun if he was to make a real impact. He introduced him to RCA Records and within weeks Elvis was signed with them.

"I was lucky"

In the early days, Elvis was asked the reason for his success. He replied, modestly, that he had been very lucky. "I came along at a time in the music business when there was no trend. The people were looking for something different and I just came along in time." However, Elvis seriously underestimated his musical ability. With hindsight, almost everyone agrees that Elvis was at his best during the years 1956 to 1958.

In January 1956, a few days after his twenty-first birthday, Elvis made his first record for RCA. *Heartbreak Hotel* rapidly became the number one record in

the United States in popularity. It was described as "echoing the strange combination of suppressed violence and self-pity that was the hallmark of the James Dean generation." James Dean was a young American actor who died tragically in a car crash in the 1950s and had become a cult figure. The record was a stark contrast to the noisy *Rock Around The Clock* by Bill Haley and the Comets, which had previously dominated the charts.

To present Elvis to an even bigger audience than the record-buying public, Colonel Parker arranged for him to appear on television in New York City. Elvis went on, swiveling his hips and snarling. He sang *Heartbreak Hotel* and another song called *Blue Suede Shoes*.

Fans became hysterical whenever Elvis appeared. They screamed, grabbed his clothes and tried to follow him to his hotel room. Despite this lack of privacy, Elvis always seemed to enjoy his fans' admiration.

Not everyone liked Elvis. The religious leader, Billy Graham, said that Elvis was not the sort of boy he would like his children to see. Others used the singer as a

The older generation found "Elvis mania" hard to understand.

scapegoat, blaming him for increasing juvenile delinquency. He was described as "vulgar" and "talentless." All this hurt Elvis, who had been brought up in a strict, religious family atmosphere, and did not wish to offend anyone.

The Elvis appeal

Elvis sang Hound Dog *to a real dog as a publicity gimmick.*

Perhaps to make Elvis more appealing to older people, he was seen on one television show singing his famous hit *Hound Dog* to a real dog. Then Ed Sullivan, the most famous man in American television at that time, booked him for three shows, paying him $50,000. Not long before, he had said, "I won't touch Elvis with a long stick."
But, he insisted that Elvis was filmed only from the waist up!
During 1956, Elvis made eleven singles, and a number of other records, and was awarded six Golden Discs. Fan clubs were growing and Elvis souvenirs, such as pencils, posters and bubble gum were manufactured. All this was masterminded by Colonel Parker. He then decided that Elvis should also be in the movies. Elvis' first film was called *Love Me Tender*, a Western. Although the fans loved it, the critics did not. Two more films followed in 1957, *Loving*

You and *Jailhouse Rock*.

As Elvis became more successful, criticism of him decreased. Ed Sullivan even called him "a real decent fine boy." And the early controversy had not damaged Elvis' career. He was becoming a very wealthy young man. In 1957, he bought the house that was to become the center of his life, a mansion called Graceland, just outside Memphis. It cost him $100,000 and he spent more on new building and the construction of a swimming pool.

Early in 1958, Elvis was due to start on his fourth film, *King Creole*. But he was drafted for military service by the U.S. Army. Colonel Parker managed to get a delay so that Elvis could make the film, but even he could not keep Elvis out of the army. As it happened, this was a duty Elvis and the Colonel had no intention of dodging.

Elvis began his career as a Rock 'n' Roll singer by signing with Sam Phillips.

The Colonel

Many people thought that when Elvis disappeared into the army he would quickly be forgotten. But Colonel Parker realized that two years in the army could be turned to Elvis' advantage. He would be recognized as a patriotic American who had done his duty, and his appeal would spread to all age groups, including older people who had previously shunned him.

Colonel Parker was not American. Research indicates that he was probably Dutch, born in 1910, and came to the United States as a teenager, changing his name. His title of Colonel was an honorary one, given to him by the Governor of Tennessee in the early 1950s.

Colonel Parker had previously worked in carnivals and circuses, attracting customers with discount tickets and other gimmicks. In his time he had worked with ponies, monkeys, dancing chickens, and sparrow disguised as canaries! Later, he promoted and managed country and western singers, but when Elvis came along, he devoted all his time to "my boy." He frequently said: "When I first knew Elvis he had a million dollars worth of talent. Now he has a million dollars."

Colonel Parker had great faith in Elvis, and worked as his full-time manager.

Graceland

A year after he bought his splendid new home, Graceland, Elvis had to leave it to join the army. The twenty-three room house was a complete contrast to the two-room shack where he had been born, and the succession of shabby homes he had shared with his parents. And it stood on several acres of land.

Elvis intended Graceland to be a real family home – he loved spending Christmas there – and spent a lot of money redesigning it to his own taste. At the entrance he installed a pair of large musical gates covered with musical figures and notes. He lived there with his parents, then his wife and daughter.

Later he became a recluse in this house, and finally died there. Elvis, his parents and grandmother are buried at Graceland. The grounds and ground floor of the house are open to visitors and many thousands come from all over the world to visit it every year.

Elvis beside the famous musical gates at the entrance to Graceland.

"Uncle Sam's boy"

In March 1958, Elvis Presley became Private U.S. 53310761. He told reporters that he was proud to serve his country as a soldier, not as an entertainer in the Army Special Services. "Whatever the army people want me to do is fine. I don't expect any special privileges or favors. Those people in the service are fair. They demand discipline and respect, and that's what I'll give them."

In the army, Elvis took a drastic pay cut, from $100,000 a month, which he got from his record company alone, to $80 a month. He also had a regulation style short-back-and-sides hair cut, losing the famous sideburns.

Priscilla Beaulieu was Elvis' girlfriend in Germany.

After six months' basic training, Elvis was posted to West Germany. He became a jeep driver, but was driven to camp each morning in a black Mercedes! Elvis took advantage of the fact that soldiers were allowed to live with nearby relatives, and rented a luxurious house for himself, his father and grandmother.

Elvis' mother had died shortly before he left for Germany. Her death distressed Elvis deeply. "Oh God, oh God, everything I have is gone," he cried at the news. Gladys had been in poor health for some time, because of her excess weight.

Yet Elvis was not unhappy while in the army. In Germany, he met a pretty fourteen-year-old, Priscilla Beaulieu, the daughter of an American air force officer. Priscilla was too young at that time for a serious romance, but seven years later she married Elvis.

Thanks to Colonel Parker, Elvis' fans had not forgotten him while he was away. The Colonel made sure there were enough recordings to keep them happy. Some had been made before Elvis joined the army, some during leave and some were reissues of past hits. There were also films and news bulletins about him.

Back from army service

When Elvis left the army in 1960, he had changed. Physically he looked leaner, his hair was much shorter and his sideburns had vanished. The famous sneer and hip movements had also gone. "Elvis," said one critic, "is the bad boy made good."

As predicted, the army had improved Elvis' image. He had gained many more fans, who approved of the new, clean-cut, all-American boy image. Elvis' records became mellower. One of his first big hits made after his return was *It's Now Or Never,* based on *O Sole Mio,* which had been made famous by Mario Lanza, an operatic tenor and actor.

Elvis' first television appearance after the army was on the Frank Sinatra Show. Sinatra had disapproved of Rock 'n' Roll and performers like Elvis, calling them "cretinous goons." Now he praised Elvis, who sang alongside him, wearing evening dress.

The old fans stayed faithful, hoping that the old Elvis would re-emerge. But Elvis was stuck in a film-making rut for almost ten years, while heroes such as The Beatles, The Who and The Rolling Stones appeared.

Elvis' films made a lot of money, but were generally disliked by critics. Elvis churned them out at a rate of three a year. They were made quickly, in a matter of weeks, were thin on plot and musically bland. By 1965, Elvis had made seventeen films, including *G I Blues, Wild in the Country, Blue Hawaii* and *Kid Galahad.*

There were very few live appearances in what came to be regarded as Elvis' declining years. He gave his last concert in 1961, and then did not make another concert or television appearance for seven years. Hit records were still produced, usually the tracks of his film scores, but even his most loyal supporters thought these lacked the excitement and drive of his earliest songs.

After he left the army, Elvis was given a warmer welcome by older people who liked his new, wholesome image.

"Just like a spoiled child"

From having nothing, Elvis rose in a few years to the man who could have anything. He was known for his great generosity, buying clothes, cars and jewelery for his friends, and for people he hardly knew. Although Colonel Parker controlled his working life, back home at Graceland, Elvis surrounded himself with a gang of close friends, known as the "Memphis Mafia." They called Elvis "The Chief." They protected him, worked for him, and offered him twenty-four-hour-a-day companionship – on Elvis' terms.

Elvis' parents, especially Gladys, had spoiled him as a child; now his friends did the same. If Elvis wanted to play football at four in the morning, that is what they did. When Elvis took up karate, they all did too. Elvis' lifestyle was bizarre – he slept during the day and played all night. His parties sometimes lasted for days.

Priscilla

On May 1, 1967, Elvis married Priscilla Beaulieu, the girl he had first met while he was in Germany. He was thirty-two and she was twenty-one. After the wedding Priscilla probably saw less of Elvis than his fans did! He was often away making films, and liked the company of his friends at home.

The couple were married in Las Vegas, with a traditional white wedding. Elvis later said that Priscilla was one of the few girls he knew who was interested in him as a person, not because he was the "King" of Rock 'n' Roll.

On February 1, 1968, their daughter, Lisa Marie, was born. Elvis adored his little girl. But he was often away from home, and when he was there, Priscilla disliked the constant presence of the "Memphis Mafia" and her husband's behavior. In 1972, she left Elvis and divorced him in 1973. They remained friends, however, and Elvis continued to see his beloved daughter.

The second comeback

In December 1968, Elvis made a television special which ended his eight year "slumber in Hollywood." The show was called *Elvis,* and for the fans who had waited so long it was a rare treat. To their delight and amazement, the old Elvis was back; he was wearing a black leather outfit, his hair was long and greasy, and there was the familiar sneer on his face. He sang all the old favorites, and joked and laughed with the audience. Even the critics were enthusiastic about the power of his voice and performance.

Elvis' second comeback was staged because his records were not selling well and audiences for his films were dwindling. Colonel Parker realized that something had to be done to maintain Elvis' popularity. Elvis promised more live appearances after this. He was in great voice and made new records which were said to be better than anything he had produced in the past five years.

In the 1970s, Elvis made a spectacular comeback on television.

Yet it was his live performances that ensured his continued popularity, and showed the world that Elvis was still the "King."

In 1969, he appeared for a month in Las Vegas, earning $150,000 a week. He wore new outfits, and was accompanied by backing groups and an orchestra. It was a different image once again, but his most loyal fans were still there.

Elvis continued to perform in Las Vegas during the 1970s. Wearing elaborate stage suits and capes – later designed to disguise his bulky figure – he became the most popular entertainer in town.

There were concerts in other cities such as New York, and celebrities like the Beatles were seen in the audience. One concert in Hawaii in 1973 was beamed by satellite to television stations all over the world. Yet by 1976, it was obvious that Elvis was almost burned out. His voice was still strong, but he often forgot his words, or looked unwell on stage. The magic of Elvis was almost gone.

His own worst enemy

After the divorce, Elvis suffered from bouts of depression. When these occurred, he ate vast quantities of "junk food." His mother had done exactly the same and, like her, Elvis put on a tremendous amount of weight in the last years of his life.

Everyone could see the physical effects of these binges, but few guessed that Elvis was addicted to pills. This addiction had begun in the army when he took them to keep him alert on maneuvers. Elvis continued taking these, and also took diet pills, sleeping pills and pain killers. He was able to get these drugs because doctors prescribed them for him without question.

Ironically, Elvis was very much against illegal "hard" drugs, like heroin. He stopped a concert in 1974 to deny that he

Elvis adored his only child, Lisa Marie, and even after the divorce he saw her as often as possible.

The burial plot of the Presley family at Graceland, in Memphis.

was taking this, and showed the audience his certificate from the International Narcotics Enforcement Association awarding him life membership.

Elvis' last few days were spent quite pleasantly. Lisa Marie was staying with him at Graceland, and one day Elvis hired an amusement park for himself and a group of friends.

At 2:30 p.m. on August 16, 1977, Elvis was discovered lying in his bathroom unconscious. He was given mouth to mouth resuscitation, then rushed to the Baptist Memorial Hospital in Memphis, where doctors tried to revive him. But, at forty-two years old, Elvis Aaron Presley was dead. Doctors announced that he had died of a heart attack. The cause of his death was never fully revealed, but it was claimed he had died of a drug overdose.

Elvis' body lay at Graceland before its burial. Over 20,000 loyal fans filed past his coffin. The American President, Jimmy Carter, said that Elvis Presley had "permanently changed the face of American popular culture." No one has ever disagreed with that tribute.

Important dates

1935   Elvis Aaron Presley born in Tupelo, Mississippi (January 8).

1948   The Presley family moves to Memphis, Tennessee.

1953   Elvis leaves school and makes a record for his mother's birthday.

1954   Elvis begins his professional singing career with Sam Phillips of the Sun Record Company.

1955   Colonel Tom Parker takes over the management of Elvis.

1956   Elvis' first television appearance.
Heartbreak Hotel reaches number one on the American charts.
Elvis makes his first film, *Love Me Tender*.

1957   Elvis buys Graceland.
Elvis receives his draft papers from the U.S. Army.

1958   Elvis joins the army.
His mother, Gladys, dies.
Elvis goes to serve in Germany.

1960   Elvis is discharged from the army.
He makes a comeback appearance on the Frank Sinatra Show.
He begins a series of films which last through the next decade.

1967   Elvis marries Priscilla Beaulieu.

1968   Their daughter, Lisa Marie, is born.
Elvis makes a comeback television spectacular.

1969   Elvis makes a successful series of appearances in Las Vegas, and appears there throughout the 1970s.

1973   Elvis is divorced from Priscilla.

1977   Elvis dies (August 16).

Books to read

Alicio, Stella H. *Elvis Presley – The Beatles.* West Haven CT: Pendulum Press, 1979.

Canada, Lena. *To Elvis with Love.* New York: Scholastic, Inc., 1979.

Harms, Valerie. *Tryin' to Get to You: The Story of Elvis Presley.* New York: Atheneum, 1979.

Lacker, Marty, et al. *Elvis: Portrait of a Friend.* Memphis, TN: Wimmer Brothers Books, 1979.

Love, Robert. *Elvis Presley.* New York: Franklin Watts, 1986.

Taylor, Paula. *Elvis Presley.* Mankato, MN: Creative Education, 1974.

Wootton, Richard. *Elvis.* New York: Random House, 1985.

Glossary

Bizarre   Fantastic or strange.

Cult   People united by admiration of, or devotion to, a person or a thing.

Deep South   The southeastern states of the U.S., especially South Carolina, Georgia, Alabama, Louisiana, and Mississippi, where Elvis was brought up.

Draft   The government of the United States required all young men to serve in the army and sent them their draft notices.

"Elvis mania"   The craze for Elvis Presley and his music.

Gimmicks   Ideas for catching people's attention, especially when selling things.

Great Depression   The worldwide economic slump of the 1930s, which caused mass unemployment.

Hysterical   Overexcited and uncontrolled behavior.

Juvenile delinquency   The anti-social, and sometimes unlawful, behaviour of some young people.

Narcotics   Drugs, intended to ease pain or induce sleep.

Prejudice   An unjustified and unreasonable point of view.

Protégé   Someone under the care and guidance of another person.

Recluse   A person who shuts himself away from other people.

Retrospect   Looking back on past activities or events.

Scapegoat   A person made to take the blame for the faults of others.

Sentimental   Influenced by feelings rather than by reason.

Stillborn   To be born dead.

Uncle Sam   A slang term for the Government of the United States.

Picture credits

John Topham cover, title page, 4, 12, 15, 21, 29; Photri 11.

Index